Ocean Animals

SEAHORSES

By Benjamin Proudfit

Gareth Stevens
PUBLISHING

Please visit our website, www.garethstevens.com. For a free color catalog of all our high-quality books, call toll free 1-800-542-2595 or fax 1-877-542-2596.

Library of Congress Cataloging-in-Publication Data

Names: Proudfit, Benjamin, author.
Title: Seahorses / Benjamin Proudfit.
Description: New York : Gareth Stevens Publishing, [2020] | Series: Ocean animals
Identifiers: LCCN 2019010485| ISBN 9781538244654 (paperback) | ISBN 9781538244678 (library bound) | ISBN 9781538244661 (6 pack)
Subjects: LCSH: Sea horses–Juvenile literature.
Classification: LCC QL638.S9 P76 2020 | DDC 597/.6798–dc23
LC record available at https://lccn.loc.gov/2019010485

First Edition

Published in 2020 by
Gareth Stevens Publishing
111 East 14th Street, Suite 349
New York, NY 10003

Copyright © 2020 Gareth Stevens Publishing

Designer: Katelyn E. Reynolds
Editor: Kristen Rajczak Nelson

Photo credits: Cover, p. 1 Kjeld Friis/Shutterstock.com; p. 5 Elena_sg80/Shutterstock.com; p. 7 Laura Dinraths/Shutterstock.com; p. 9 Rich Carey/Shutterstock.com; pp. 11, 24 (fin) Arunee Rodloy/Shutterstock.com; pp. 13, 24 (plates) Oksana Maksymova/Shutterstock.com; pp. 15, 24 (tail) Chanita Chokchaikul/Shutterstock.com; p. 17 Mike Workman/Shutterstock.com; p. 19 Nora Tam/South China Morning Post via Getty Images; p. 21 (top left) kaschibo/Shutterstock.com; p. 21 (top right) Cherdchai Chaivimol/Shutterstock.com; p. 21 (bottom left) Charlotte Bleijenberg/Shutterstock.com; p. 21 (bottom right) Fiona Ayerst/Shutterstock.com; p. 23 Decha Somparn/Shutterstock.com.

Printed in the United States of America

Some of the images in this book illustrate individuals who are models. The depictions do not imply actual situations or events.

CPSIA compliance information: Batch #CW20GS: For further information contact Gareth Stevens, New York, New York at 1-800-542-2595.

Contents

Seahorses live
in the ocean!

They are found
near coasts.

They live in warm water.

They are fish.
They have fins.

They are covered
in plates.

They have tails.
Their tails can hold on!

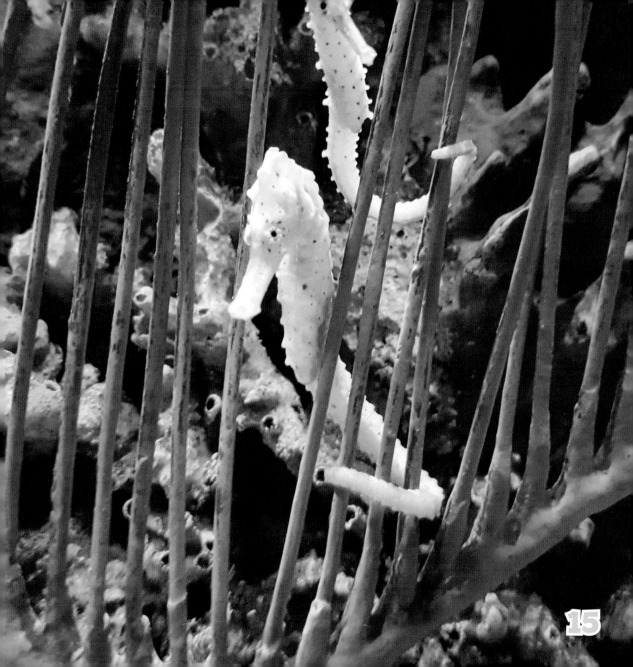

They eat shrimp.

Lots of babies are born at once!